INTERCEPTED
SIGNS
&
REINCARNATION

ASTROLOGY & REINCARNATION

Part I

Retrograde Planets and Reincarnation

PART II

Intercepted Signs and Reincarnation

PART III

Triangulation of Saturn/Jupiter/Mercury

Astrology and Reincarnation   Volume 2

INTERCEPTED SIGNS & REINCARNATION

by
DONALD H. YOTT

assisted by
ANNE ROGERS

SAMUEL WEISER INC.   NEW YORK

Samuel Weiser, Inc.
625 Broadway
N.Y., N.Y. 10012

ISBN 0-87728-374-5

Printed in the
United States of America
by Noble Offset Printers, Inc.
New York City

CONTENTS

An intercepted sign occurs when a sign is contained entirely within a house but does not appear on either cusp. Interceptions can occur in any system of house division except the Equal House System which was designed, in part, to avoid having interceptions.

Unlike retrogradation, interception is not an observable phenomena. It occurs because of the shape of the Earth and the tilt of its axis (approximately 23°) to the path that the Earth follows in its revolution around the Sun. In horoscopes of people born close to the equator, each house contains nearly 30° with distortions of only a degree or two. But further north or south from the equator, this distortion becomes greater and the house projections into the heavens expand and diminish with the curvature of the Earth, producing an 'accordion' effect. Some houses may then contain much more than 30° and when this happens, there is the possibility that a sign will fall totally between adjacent house cusps. These are called intercepted signs. Intercepted signs always occur in pairs, the opposite sign being intercepted, too. For example, if Aries is intercepted in the first house, then Libra will be intercepted in the seventh house.

G. Courey

INTERCEPTED SIGNS

Astrology today is becoming more scientifically based. Up to the present, much of astrology has been confined to that which has been handed down through the centuries. Many terms in astrology have not been clearly defined and now must be. There must be more of a universality in meaning; there are too many conflicting schools of thought and no central authority to finalize their differences.

Astrologers are not scientific enough. There is a pattern that has been worked out since the time of creation. It isn't by chance that two planets within three degrees of each other are considered a conjunction or that a sign is intercepted and that the word "intercepted" is used. It is in the study of language that astrologers often cause confusion. They should be very much concerned with words and their meanings. If we use the word "conjunction", we mean to co-join. If we employ the word "intercepted", we mean something is being interfered with.

In particular with interceptions, there are two schools of thought in astrology. One school declares that an interception is a focal point in a horoscope and much attention should be placed on it and its qualities. The other school of thought states that interceptions are not important and too weak to take into consideration.

When we use the word "interception", we mean that something has come between the constellation and the Earth. It isn't that the influence is weakened, but it is not coming through as clearly and, of course, we are always concerned with the influence as related to the qualities of the Sun.

Part of our job as incarnating human beings is to develop all of the signs of the zodiac in the affairs of the houses, and as we come in, lifetime after lifetime, we will for example, experience Virgo in the first or second or third house. This is because we must perfect ourselves in all areas of life through all the qualities of the signs. When an intercepted sign is in a chart, it indicates that the influence is there but is having difficulty finding a channel of expression. We could say that one school is right in that the influence might be considered weak. The other school is also right in saying that it is a focal point, for any weakness should be an area to which we must pay attention because we must transmute our weaknesses into strengths. From an esoteric viewpoint, and from the viewpoint of reincarnation and Karma, an intercepted sign means that we neglected to develop or to grow through the qualities of that sign in the affairs of that house in other lifetimes. It was serious neglect on our part and so in this lifetime we must develop and incorporate these qualities. But the interception causes problems — obstacles which are really channels of opportunities.

Most Karma, when it is negative, is brought about by a refusal to acept our duties. We take energies and we misuse them. We pervert them or we neglect them; thus is Karma built up. An intercepted sign means we neglected to develop the qualities of the sign and it isn't that we neglected it in one lifetime only, but in several lifetimes. Because of this we will find that intercepted signs often bring out circumstances in our lives which are beyond our control. In the main, these circumstances aren't obvious. The word "intercepted" itself, means that something is interfered with or isn't clearly seen. We really can't "see" the sign and there is a hidden, subtle force in our present lifetime. This evidences itself as a gap in our life, something missing, a hidden something that we seem to be searching for and just can't put our finger on.

All intercepted signs represent these circumstances beyond our control and, in relation to reincarnation and Karma, these are the circumstances which you neglected to fulfill in past lifetimes. As an example of this, let us suppose that there is an intercepted Virgo somewhere in the chart. It indicates that, first of all, many people will demand our service. It is the sign of service; it is the sign of discrimination; it is the sign of the teacher. When we have an intercepted Virgo, people will always be calling upon us, needing our help, always seeking our advice and we have no control over it. It just seems as if all of this gravitates towards us. The reason is that in past lifetimes, we were not of service and ignored cries for assistance. People sought our advice and we could not be bothered with any kind of guidance or counseling in the past.

Virgo is the natural ruler of the house of service and the public, and so when you have an intercepted Virgo, you neglected to give help, assistance, the shoulder for someone to lean on in other lifetimes, in the area of the chart where it is intercepted.

If we have an intercepted sign, we should look back over the pattern of our life and we should be able to see where this has been working from the viewpoint of service. Most of our Karma, then, is the result of neglect or the avoidance of responsibilities. We have to look to the main qualities or features of the sign. There are more qualities about Virgo than discrimination, service and teaching. When it comes to reincarnation, we must point to the main qualities or the major qualities of Virgo. Remember one thing: we are not and never should be slaves or automatons to our charts. But we *have* made the chart; we entered this life through past deeds and experiences. What we have made, we can unmake; we can outlive and outgrow our chart at any time, once we are aware of it. In esoteric astrology, it is thought that once we arrive at the level of esoteric astrology and know it, and use it, we no longer need our chart for we have become the master of our destiny.

Remember, too, our whole chart is the result of reincarnation and Karma; it is karmicly oriented and based. We do not consider only intercepted signs or retrograde planets, for the chart represents the sum total of all our lives.

When the soul realizes it is time to reincarnate and searches for a body being created, it desires a time when the stars in the heavens will be in certain positions. These will be the guideposts creating the opportunities and challenges to work off Karma and to have the necessary experiences for new developments in life. Each life then grants us opportunities to work for the future. We are always reaping Karma, and the reaping of Karma is the opportunity, but we are sowing Karma at the same time.

Intercepted signs will usually bring out negative rather than positive traits because of the fact that we neglected them in the past. Since it is more difficult to bring out the qualities of intercepted signs, we might tend to be too passive, to follow along with the stream of life insofar as these signs are concerned. Negative qualities seem to have more emphasis with intercepted signs than the positive. If we focus attention on our negative qualities, we can transmute them. These are the areas through which we learn the greatest lessons in life. If you have an intercepted sign, naturally the opposite sign is intercepted. These we must correlate. One will always be in the southern part of the chart, the other in the bottom or the northern part of the chart. One is in the "I" area; the other in the "We". Our charts represent polarity. The whole key to life is polarity or balance and the center of our chart is where the balance is achieved. That is why, on a mundane level, the Pars Fortuna is in the center of the chart because that is where we are — on Earth. The Earth represents material life — dense, gross, physical matter — and we must balance the material aspect of life with the spiritual. So, always, we need balance and this is where we should be striving. Balance means harmony and harmony is a higher interpretation of the word "love", and love is the basic principle of creation. That is what started it all. Intercepted signs are very important for very few people are aggressive enough in their lives to make an effort to change negative traits. In order to bring out the qualities of an intercepted sign, we have to work at it harder. The tendency might be to be too passive, very similar to someone with a chart which has more positive than negative aspects. A chart that is too well aspected can be more of a burden than a chart with many negative aspects. This is because things could come too easily and there isn't enough balance. We can become too passive about life. We should bless our negative aspects — they are our opportunities for growth. They represent our challenges. However, do not ever neglect the good aspects — they are the helpers. They can be little crutches to help us to transmute the negative qualities or to take negative aspects and learn how to use their energies.

A negative aspect represents energies as much as a positive aspect. Electricity is the result of a negative and positive charge. We could never have electric light with just negative or just positive charges. We cannot develop and learn and become spiritualized beings until we learn to balance and utilize both the positive and negative influences in our lives. On an esoteric level, we realize that the negative aspects are tremendous opportunities for growth and the positive represent what we have already accomplished and can be the crutches or the railing on the steps. We can only grow through balance.

We do not always grow when everything is going well. When we look back at crises, we find that the crises and challenges have made us what we are. The obstacles make us grow, but in the long run, it is the effort that is so very, very, important.

ARIES-LIBRA

Wendy

Aries intercepted in the first house, Libra in the seventh.

What are we concerned with here? The main quality of Aries, from the viewpoint of reincarnation, being in the first house, implies the neglect of the proper development of the "I", the ego. It is very necessary in life that we become self-aware — that we develop the quality of awareness. Aries is also aggressive. Arians are leaders and organizers. In a negative way, they can be very impatient with others who do not learn as quickly as they do, or those who do not do as well. Now the intercepted quality of Aries would indicate that these negative traits were more prominent — impatience with others, lack of the development of self-awareness. The self-awareness development, by reaction to Libra for balance, shoould have been from the viewpoint of "We", from the viewpoint of concern and consideration for others. We did not develop the proper personality in the past which should have reflected not only ourselves but ourselves as we identified with others. The intercepted quality of Aries here would emphasize that we were too concerned with ourselves first. It also tells that we did not use or try to develop qualities of leadership. Since Pisces would be on the cusp of the first house, we could possibly have been very passive about life and our participation in life, taking too much for granted, and not appreciating other people enough. Now the lesson to learn with an intercepted Aries in the first house is to place our attention upon developing a personality to the extent that it would be at-one with all of manifested life. Instead of "me first", it would be "after you".

The intercepted sign of Libra would be in the seventh house. This represents balance between the "I" and the "We". It implies that you were not balanced and this further emphasizes the need for the development of the Aries qualities which should function by reaction in Libra. Librans are intellectually inclined, graceful, interested in refined and cultural things, and they love peace and

6

harmony. They appreciate art and music on all levels. In a negative way, the Libran can be the troublemaker. The Libran can also pervert artistic tastes into low, crude forms. So the interception of Libra could imply that where others were concerned and also with our relationship to life, we created disharmony rather than harmony. We did not develop the proper interests in more cultural, intellectual and spiritual activities. We could have been very gross, crude and ill-mannered in the past. There is even a certain degree of snobbery with the involved negative Libra.

The lesson of the intercepted signs of Aries-Libra is to solve the problem of balance so that we can achieve at-one-ment. Each sign represents the beginning of two very important quartiles and, eventually, through the I-We fulfillment, we can arrive at universality.

Aries intercepted in the second house, Libra in the eighth

Here the intercepted sign of Aries is related to values, to material things, to money, to security. But on an esoteric level, it is related to the value of ourselves. What it implies, being intercepted in the second house, is that we failed to develop in the past the proper values; the proper value of ourselves, the proper value of others. We placed too much attention on the external features of life as being the all-important ones. The Libra intercepted in the eighth house indicates again the need for balance and shows that we did not appreciate the higher things of life. We neglected to develop interest in intellectual pursuits and spiritual activities. The affairs of the eighth house involve the search for truth, reality, and metaphysics. There was the neglect of effort on the part of the Libra to become involved in these activities.

The lesson of Libra here is that involvement in these activities could produce peace and harmony for the Libran and for others. The balance with Aries would indicate that effort made through the qualities of Libra could stimulate the leadership and organizational abilities that we have. These were neglected in past lifetimes and we must now become leaders in higher activities of living.

Another example of this Aries-Libra interception, in the

eighth house, could be that we neglected to assume the responsibilities and respect for other people's possessions, or for their money, or for things in general.

Aries intercepted in the third house, Libra in the ninth.

This interception implies that the individual neglected to develop the proper means of communication with others; he neglected to develop a body of knowledge through which he could instruct or share with others. It also shows that we failed to develop skills or training on an educational level. We did not develop the proper communication where our neighbors or our brothers and sisters were concerned. But one must always remember that everyone in the world is a brother or sister to us. We also neglected to develop the quality of patience when it came to teaching others, and we failed to develop patience about ourselves in relationship to life. It also implies that we neglected to use our practical, everyday mind (Mercury) and we did not achieve self-identification. We could have been self-aware, but we did not to add the quality of self-identification with others.

The third house represents the fulfillment of the "I" and by opposition to the ninth house, the fulfillment of the "We". The Libra intercepted in the ninth house shows neglect in developing the higher mind or that too much attention was centered on the mundane, practical level. It also represents the neglect of the fulfillment of the "We" from the viewpoint of a spiritualized being. The Libra could also imply that we had been exposed to higher Truth teachings, philosophy, religion, etc., but did not use them properly, investigating them merely from curiosity rather than for their application to life.

The sign of Libra dictates that we have a partnership with life and must apply all knowledge and experience to life.

This interception of Aries and Libra in the third and ninth houses shows the neglect of the self-identification and the "We" so that fulfillment of both concepts could be accomplished.

We neglected to balance ourselves in the third quartile with others in the third quartile.

Aries intercepted in the fourth house, Libra in the tenth.

The Aries qualities here indicate that you neglected to use your personality and leadership qualities in influencing and affecting others. You had the opportunities of leaving your mark upon the world and neglected to make the effort to do so.

Aries in the fourth house shows that we neglected to apply self-awareness and self-identification in the experiences of life. The application of self-identification or self-awareness to life initiates the final stages preparatory to our entrance into the "We" concept. Thus, through our neglect, we could not identify self with others and, until we achieve this, we cannot assist, counsel or guide others.

An intercepted Aries in the fourth house tells that we neglected helping others, and did not give the guidance and counsel so needed by others in our environment.

Libra intercepted in the tenth house indicates the neglect in assuming responsibilities of authority. Here is the individual who could have been instrumental as a mediator in disputes in organizational affairs. The tendency here could have been towards non-involvement and the Libra shows the neglect of being involved.

This neglect of authority could also have carried over into parenthood by not assuming the responsibilities of being a proper parent. The intercepted Libra also would imply that we lacked self-discipline in the past.

Aries intercepted in the fifth house, Libra in the eleventh.

We are most concerned here with the lack of development or use of the qualities of creativity. On certain mundane levels, we could also determine that we neglected children in the past by not caring for their needs, by not giving proper direction, by not loving. We may have neglected our moral responsibilities to those with whom we were involved in love affairs.

The Libra, intercepted in the eleventh house, shows that we did not develop proper relationships in a creative manner with everyone. Some of the intellectual snobbery of Libra could easily have entered the picture here, making us tend to associate only with those who had our interests, rather than with everyone.

The eleventh house position of an intercepted Libra also implies the neglect of intellectual and spiritual influence upon others. Here we have the balance of the fourth quartile at stake and, by neglecting to develop the proper relationships with others, we could easily have failed in achieving the ideal of brotherhood.

Libra is the most idealistic sign in the zodiac and its interception in the eleventh house implies the neglect of ideals in our associations with others. The balance of Aries and Libra as intercepted signs in the fifth and eleventh houses requires creative relationships, intellectually and spiritually applied in our everyday contacts. There are moral values involved here that were neglected in the past.

Aries intercepted in the sixth house, Libra in the twelfth.

The problem here is the person neglected to relate to the public.

He did not see himself as a leader nor did he become involved in the problems of others. The "I am" was rather selfishly emphasized and shows a tremendous amount of self-centeredness. The quality of service was lacking. One did not develop the personality to the point where there would be a rapport between one's self and the public, so service in relationship to others was neglected in the past.

Since the sixth house is the natural location of Virgo it could mean that the individual was far too concerned with his own personal well-being, and especially his health, because a Virgo can be a hypochondriac.

Since Libra begins the "We" concept, it shows that the individual has reached the point in spiritual development and intellectual understanding of being able to unite with, or function through, the ideal of brotherhood. This would be the fulfillment of the "We", but since Libra is intercepted, there was something missing — the person did not take that final step of complete brotherhood, or complete universality.

As Pisces is the natural ruler here, it would indicate that the final Initiation towards this fulfillment was not successfully passed or the person neglected to take it. Remember, intercepted signs always imply the neglect of the development of the quality of the sign in the affairs of the house.

Aries intercepted in the seventh house, Libra in the first.

The native neglected to take others into consideration and there was little concern for others. With business partners, marriage partners, or life, he came first. He failed to identify himself with others, which is the main development of Aries on the cusp of the 7th, anyway. This is the goal with this location of Aries.

Libra in the first house emphasizes this lack of identification with others because, here, the individual neglected to incorporate the "We" concept into the development of the personality.

This would put Scorpio on the cusp of the first house, so there would be an aloofness, a snobbery in the personality.

Libra intercepted in the first house indicates that the individual was snobbish in the past and neglected to develop the quality of concern and consideration for others. Of major importance to this individual was the manner in which the world saw him. Consequently, he did not have the type of personality which encouraged people to come to him, or the type of presence in which others would feel comfortable. In some cases, this interception of Libra could indicate a disorganized personality.

Aries intercepted in the eighth house, Libra in the second.

Aries, in this location, is more involved on a spiritual and esoteric level than on a mundane level, though it will also function on the mundane physical level. Primarily, the Aries attitude would indicate that the person neglected to concern himself with any search for truth. He was too interested in his own material and physical security and less with intellectual and spiritual matters.

There was neglect in trying to determine or locate for himself a true meaning to life or to find a proper direction. The values the person had were not of a higher nature when it came to truth or life.

Libra intercepted shows the lack of appreciation for material things on a level other than just as material possessions. With Libra in the second house, the individual should have developed a fine appreciation for things as they are used in life and the full meaning behind possessions and security. He would mainly have been concerned with his own things and less with how things could be used in relationship to others.

Brian

Aries intercepted in the ninth house, Libra in the third.

Here is the "I am" in relationship to higher knowledge, religion, philosophy. The intercepted Aries here indicates the individual failed to relate himself to a workable philosophy of life that was constructive. He did not develop a broadness of vision.

The Arian tends to be rather impatient with others who don't learn as quickly or cannot do things as well as he. There was a lack of understanding and a lack of granting to others the freedom of expression in the past.

With Libra in the third house, the person failed to develop the proper means of communication with others. This is probably the most important lack of development on the part of Libra in the past because Libra is concerned with "We".

The third house represents communication so Libra intercepted in the third shows that this individual did not develop the proper means of communicating with others. Thus the "we" concept in communication did not come to fruition. Also, he was not interested in travel.

Aries intercepted in the tenth house, Libra in the fourth.

There is a direct correlation between the Aries and the Libra because both the tenth and fourth houses, on a higher octave level, imply the manner in which we impress ourselves upon the world. What mark do we leave upon others or upon our environment? How do we influence others? What effect do we have? Aries intercepted shows that no matter where we were in our work, in government or anything else, we did not try to develop the proper personality and there was a reserve. An Aries should be an aggressive person, an organizer, a leader. Here the person failed to assume leadership, whether in government or in a profession. He failed to organize, and to be an organizer is very important in life. When we come in as Aries or with planets in Aries we have the obligation to organize things in life, to be doers. So here is a person who failed to do, in the past, and took the path of least resistence. Pisces on the tenth cusp indicates again the avoidance of responsibilities.

Libra intercepted in the fourth house, shows the person failed to accept the responsibility of influencing others. Again, the "we" concept. The Libra was not concerned and did not consider others or their problems. He remained aloof. Libra intercepted in the fourth house puts Virgo on the cusp of the fourth. Virgos can be very discriminative, prejudiced and critical and are apt to judge too quickly, whereas Libra brings the balance. Here the person was out of balance. He did not see that he had the responsibility of working with others and influencing them constructively. No matter who comes into our sphere of influence, we have the obligation of trying to influence that person (not that we are missionaries, you understand). If we are in the company of people who have a great deal more to offer than we do, then we take. But with people less evolved, less learned, less spiritual, then we have to give. With Libra intercepted, it was the failure to give of self so you could be of assistance to your fellow man or all units of manifested life.

In this case, I feel the fourth predominates over the tenth. It shows direction, and purpose in life which we can actually make manifest through tenth house affairs.

Aries intercepted in the eleventh house, Libra in the fifth.

The eleventh house represents our relationships with people, therefore the person failed to develop proper relationships with others. He avoided the responsibilities of being a leader among people, whether among friends in his social life or in any situation where he was relating to others. All of life is based on relationships. This person failed in his responsibility of developing the proper relationships with others. There was too much concern with self and self advancement, even possibly at the expense of others.

Libra intercepted in the fifth house concerns itself with creativity more than with anything else. Here the Libra shows we failed to develop the quality of "we" concerning our relationship with others. Here, again, was a selfishness. Libra indicates that one of the things we must do is to find creative approaches in our relationships with others. Intercepted here it indicates the person did not create an atmosphere of peace and harmony in establishing relationships with others. This would be on a mundane level with everyday affairs.

It is interesting that Mars being the ruler of Aries always implies on the level of reincarnation and Karma, that we work off our karma in the everyday details of life. So here we are shown that the Libra did not create peace and harmony, no matter where he went in past lifetimes, in all of the little things of life.

Aries intercepted in the twelfth house, Libra in the sixth.   *Kelly*

Here is the "I am" concept again and the failure of relating or identifying self with the all. Here is the house of the soul, where soul qualities are developed and incorporated into the general character of the person. In failing to develop the soul qualities and be the reflection of them, the person failed to develop the ideal of brotherhood and universality. Cosmic consciousness could have been accomplished had the person done what he should have in the past, in the twelfth house. Any negative quality in the twelfth house is always related to initiation, because this is the house of initiation. The person did not necessarily fail an initiation but failed to develop qualities that would lead to one, and so he never arrived at the point where the initiation was given, but he should have.

Had the Aries actually developed the soul qualities within and had he become aware of these soul qualities and identified himself with them, he would automatically have reflected brotherhood and universality. But he didn't develop these soul qalities, so the initiation which grants us universal consciousness was never given to the individual. We can't receive an initiation if we have not earned it. We didn't earn the initiation which would have granted brotherhood, universality, cosmic consciousness. There is a difference in not being given the initiation and failing it. You achieve a point in your development where you are given initiation. You either pass it or you fail it. It is similar to a test. But if you don't develop the qualities where you earn the initiation, you are not given the initiation. And why wasn't the initiation given? Libra intercepted in the sixth house — failure to be of service, failure to recognize the needs of others, failure to identify yourself with mankind, humanity. And, of course, Libra is always involved with the intellect and spirituality. So the person did not function through his intellect or through any spiritual approach in service to others.

We have a very difficult time becoming aware of ourselves. That is why throughout all metaphysical teachings we are told: "Man, know thyself." Once knowing self, you can then relate that self to life and, in the relationship of self to life, you then relate to others. There can be a superficial awareness of self, but it is never fully identified until it is put into practice and use. What good is any knowledge unless you can apply it to life. It has no value, otherwise.

TAURUS-SCORPIO

Taurus intercepted in the first house, Scorpio in the seventh.

Taureans are artistic, creative, stubborn, argumentative, materialistic, love things, values, and are possessive. The opposite of this is Scorpio — here is your conservative. Taurus is outgoing, extroverted, but Scorpio is introverted. A Scorpio is concerned with security in the same way as the Taurean, but where the Taurean will measure and value things according to what he has and what you have (and obviously so by always telling you what he paid for something), Scorpio will never let you know. The Scorpio will hoard and have things in the bank or in the vault, where a Taurean will wear all the diamonds she has. Scorpios are reserved, conservative, very suspicious, jealous, possessive in their own way, and they do carry grudges. The Taurean will smack you down and then pick you up, and say, "Let's not do this anymore," until the next time.

Taurus failed in previous lifetimes to value personality, to value the proper *development* of personality, so that the world would see him in a constructive way. He failed to value personality from the viewpoint of how he would present himself to the world. He couldn't care less.

Taurus intercepted in the first house would put Aries on the cusp of the first house, so you could well have had a very aggressive personality in the past with little concern as to how that personality affected others.

Scorpio intercepted in the seventh house shows a conservative reaction where life was concerned, where others were concerned, and an aloofness from involvement with others. It indicates thinking in terms of one's own problems.

This interception would give inner conflicts to the individual because Libra on the cusp of the seventh house would want involvement and Scorpio would not. Libra, remember, is "we", where we begin to become aware of how we should consider others. The Scorpio would tend to want to sit back and not get involved. So there is the lack of the development of involvement in the affairs of the world and with other people when Scorpio is intercepted in the seventh house.

It must also be remembered that this is the beginning of the southern portion of the chart so there would be a lack of values or involvement in intellectual and spiritual aspects of life.

Taurus intercepted in the second house, Scorpio in the eighth.

These are the houses in which these signs are the natural rulers. This would doubly emphasize the problems involved. Taurus intercepted here shows that the individual had not developed the proper attitude towards the physical world. He failed to see that materialism has its place in life according to how it is used. He failed to establish proper values for things. Undoubtedly, this individual was too much concerned with possessions as they reflected his own success in life because this is the house of money.

The Scorpio in the eighth house, on its higher octave, neglected involvement (we are still in that southern part of the chart of involvement) in the higher values of life which would include a search for truth, metaphysics, astrology, understanding reincarnation, because they are the affairs of the dead. On a mundane level, he could have refused to accept the responsibilities where other people's things were concerned. But more than anything else, Scorpio intercepted would indicate that the person had been exposed to metaphysics in the past but neglected to do anything about it. Undoubtedly, in this lifetime there would be some inner urge, or an awareness of something lacking in his life. He will always be searching, never finding. Whatever the person wants would be just beyond reach. This is the karma involved with the intercepted Scorpio.

Taurus intercepted in the third house, Scorpio in the ninth.

This situation indicates a lack of appreciation for education, for acquiring knowledge, for developing the proper means of communication. There was bluntness of speech and a narrowness in the mind's development. Here, we are concerned with the stubborn mental quality of Taurus. A Taurean becomes very self-opinionated and will not listen to what other people think. This was all part of the narrowness of the Taurean in the past.

Scorpio intercepted in the ninth house is a direct reflection of this Taurus. The individual had many opportunities for higher education, for pursuing an intellectual approach to life that would have been coupled with understanding. It would also bring in, from the past, the lack of development of broadness of mind, showing prejudice and bias. This is the individual karma of Scorpio relating to the lack of developing a proper philosophy, higher learning and an awareness of the Christ principle within, in the past. Pluto represents our own individual karma, and on its highest level or higher octave, Pluto implies that the regeneration of the individual in relationship to the ninth house afffairs was neglected.

Also, Scorpio did not grant freedom of expression to others in the past.

Taurus intercepted in the fourth house, Scorpio in the tenth.

This interception indicates a lack of interest concerning the individual's influence on others. This is the type of person who went through life caring very little about what he did or said and how it affected others. Remember, Taurus rules the throat and voice. He could say all kinds of things, hurting others and caring less. How he left his mark on the world was something he cared very little about. There was a lack of development of values in relationship to this.

This puts Scorpio intercepted in the tenth house, again by reaction to the fourth house. Here is the type of person who, in his profession or career, worked just because it was a job, for the sake of the dollar, not for what he could contribute to the job. What did he have to offer to his profession? What did he have to offer in his career? In what way did he become an authority in something so that people would turn to him for information? All he did in the past was work for the sake of how much he could get out of it, not how much he could give. Here, too, was a lack of values.

Taurus intercepted in the fifth house, Scorpio in the eleventh.

What values did the Taurean have in the past when it came to being creative? Was he artistic by nature? Did he use his creative ability and talent? Did he develop the proper relationships where others were concerned? More than anything else the fifth house is concerned with creativity. Intercepted Taurus in the fifth house indicates the failure to be creative in the past, whether along some artistic line, such as painting or singing, or in relationships with others.

Scorpio in the eleventh house shows the lack of development of values in social life, with friends and relationships. Here is the conservative from the past, reserving his personality and character for just a select few and not relating to the overall picture of mankind. Here is snobbery at its best (or worst!). On a higher octave, Scorpio could have been very spiritual, very intellectual, very understanding and compassionate, but none of these qualities were developed in the past when Scorpio is intercepted in the eleventh house.

The Scorpio and Taurus here emphasize again the values to be placed on creative abilities, creative approaches to life, and the value of our relationships.

Taurus intercepted in the sixth house, Scorpio in the twelfth.

Taurus here shows the lack of values where service to others was concerned. Service, in the past, may have been rendered, but it was from the viewpoint of how much the person got out of it, and how it gave him prestige. This was the type of person who could have been in the public limelight, not so much because of his love of service to mankind, but because by being out in front he would gain personal adulation from others.

Scorpio itself, on the cusp of the twelfth house, is always related to past karmic debts that were not worked off and initiations which failed. So an intercepted Scorpio here indicates the individual did not value his own approach to life, his own understanding of life, his own understanding of mankind, so that he could work off karma. He did not develop the full potential of his soul. He did not develop the appreciation of brotherhood. The snobbery quality of Scorpio was also evident.

Taurus intercepted in the seventh house, Scorpio in the first.

Taurus, here, stresses the lack of the development of values, consideration, and concern for others. It indicates an ego that was conceited and self-centered. In other words, the Taurus intercepted did not value the "we" concept. It was all "I" and me-first, and then you.

Scorpio intercepted in the first house shows the lack of the development of an extroverted personality in the past. It indicates the tendency to be withdrawn, conservative, and sort of a mystery. No one could possibly know this person in the past. We must not hold ourselves aloof from our fellow man. This position is directly opposite the seventh house of "we", so this individual would have lived solely from the center of self, rather than for others.

Taurus intercepted in the eighth house, Scorpio in the second.

This, again, shows the lack of the development of values in a search for the meaning to life. We did not value our relationships with others and, also, lacked values where metaphysics were concerned. This individual failed to rejuvenate himself from the viewpoint of higher truth teachings.

With Scorpio intercepted in the second house, instead of having higher values where things and possessions and life were concerned, this person measured all things according to material value. Whether it was a thing or a person, it had to have value for the individual in terms of his security. Even if a person was concerned, an intercepted Scorpio in the second house would not have valued him unless that person offered some advantage. Here, again, more value was attached to material life, less to the spiritual, and this created imbalance.

Taurus intercepted in the ninth house, Scorpio in the third.

Taurus intercepted here indicates the lack of the development of a philosophy of life and wisdom. This person did not grant to others freedom for self-expression. Would the Taurus in the past have fully appreciated the true meaning of the Christ concept, the love — wisdom philosophy? Would he be able to apply this philosophy to life and thus detach himself from self-centeredness? It is a self-centered sign and an ego-centered sign, as well. The Taurean interception did not develop an appreciation for knowledge as it could be applied to life.

Scorpio intercepted in the third house shows this person did not develop proper communication where others were concerned because of a reserve within, an unwillingness to share self with others, to share confidences with others. The intercepted Scorpio in the past held most people in contempt and couldn't be bothered communicating with others. This is the person living in the neighborhood and keeping every neighbor at arm's distance, never getting involved in their problems, never offering to help a neighbor in distress, but also never asking for help either. These are improper attitudes from the past.

Taurus intercepted in the tenth house, Scorpio in the fourth.

Taurus intercepted in the tenth house relates to values concerning whatever skill the person had developed and whether or not that skill was used in a constructive manner for the rest of mankind. Here we have the person who developed a skill purely from the viewpoint of what's-in-it-for-me and not what can I contribute to my work for the further development of it. The skill was developed for prestige, because the tenth house is ruled by Capricorn and Capricorns like prestige. This Taurean could have been the type who went into the work because of the prestige involved more than for how he could influence and affect the rest of mankind.

Scorpio intercepted in the fourth house relates to the influence and the effect we have upon other people. In the past, Scorpio couldn't have cared less about influencing or affecting others. This was the type of person who would say, "I have my problems, you have yours. You keep yours, and I'll keep mine. Don't bother me." Involvement in helping others, counselling others, being the shoulder upon which people could lean or could cry — these qualities were not developed in the past. There was too much aloofness and not enough involvement in life and the affairs of the world. No matter where this person went, he could have been creating a tremendous impact upon his fellowman, but he neglected to do so.

Taurus intercepted in the eleventh house, Scorpio in the fifth.

With Taurus intercepted in the eleventh house, what values did this person put on friends in the past? Here is the person who didn't develop any values where people were concerned as friends. This would be the fair-weather type of friend with no sincerity or loyalty in friendship or in the quality of relationship. Relationships and friendships would have been developed from the viewpoint of what he could get out of them, not what he could give to them. This person would have gathered friends around him for money and prestige, and would have been the type of person who would bask in the reflected glory of that prestige or money.

With Scorpio intercepted in the fifth house, the individual did not develop creative abilities at all. No creative approaches were developed towards anyone in his environment or towards anyone with whom he came into contact. There was a degree of snobbery. Would the intercepted Scorpio care whether he understood other people or could understand the differences that existed among men, and appreciate them? In the past, he did not and now he must. Remember that intercepted signs are focal points for development in this lifetime.

Taurus intercepted in the twelfth house, Scorpio in the sixth.

With Taurus in the twelfth house, very little value was placed on any soul qualities or the displaying of soul qualities. The ego was too strong. The soul requires humility and Taurus did not develop humility in the past, and thus did not develop the awareness of soul. Nor was he aware of his own responsibilities when it came to karma, universality or brotherhood. He was all self and everything had to relate to the material aspects of life, not the spiritual. He failed to develop the transmutation of materialism into spirituality.

Scorpio intercepted in the sixth house indicates service is involved and here again is the snobbery or the conservativism of the Scorpio. A Scorpio is either conservative or he is a snob, never in-between. If he was conservative, there would be a withdrawn quality so the lack of involvement in service to others could be because of an inferiority complex or because the person just didn't want to be bothered or didn't want to assume the responsibility. If he was a snob, he would hold the public in general in contempt. He would not be able to identify himself with the needs of the common man or social movements of the time where the evolvement of mankind was concerned.

Intercepted signs are always surrounded by two other signs picking up their qualities. There should be an attempt at balance of the three, but I haven't figured that out. Taurus intercepted has Aries and Gemini, so Taurus could be developed through the recognition of the I AM, the value of it, through the mental qualities of Gemini.

Aries is cardinal, Taurus is fixed, and Gemini is mutable, or self-values-communications. Self, awareness of self, the identification of the self-awarness. The *value* of communication with the self-identification. Self-identification is as valueless as knowledge is, unless it is applied.

GEMINI & SAGITTARIUS

Gemini intercepted in the first house, Sagittarius in the seventh.

Gemini intercepted in the first house indicates the type of person in the past who did not develop the mental, logical approach to the development of self and the awareness of self. This individual neglected the incorporation of the "We" concept in the "I Am". Because of the Gemini characteristic he lacked the quality of continuity, which is one of the failures of the Gemini. Gemini tends to be unemotional and aloof, but the most important quality of Gemini is the development of the mind. Since mind is both mental and spiritual, the mind quality should be part of the attribute of personality. Here was personality, without the mental attribute. Taurus and Cancer surround Gemini, contributing to the lack of value where mind was concerned and a tendency toward being too emotional in the past.

Sagittarius intercepted in the seventh house is a mental sign, indicating the tendency to be too dogmatic in the past, seeing the world in relation to yourself, rather than yourself in relation to the world. Since it is an ego-centered sign. there was a neglect of incorporating the "I" with the "We". There was no concern or consideration for others in the past. Since the seventh house represents a partnership in life, there was little identification of self with life. This is because of the reaction to Gemini ruled by Mercury: Mercury is involved on an esoteric level with the principle of self-identification. In the past, you lacked faith when it came to relationship with life itself.

Gemini intercepted in the second house, Sagittarius in the eighth.

This represents the involvement with values where your mind was concerned. What value did you have towards mental accomplishments or achievements? There was little concern given to the development of the quality of imagination, and since the glyph of Gemini represents the two streams of life, the material and the spiritual, there was no balance developed from this viewpoint. It could easily be that you were too materialistic in the past, that mental activities were geared towards security and possessions. Or, alternatively, the imaginative faculties could have been used in daydreaming and fantasy, lacking practical application.

Sagittarius, here, is intercepted in the eighth house. Here the search for truth was accomplished through an ego-centeredness. You saw truth only as it related to yourself. You could easily have used segments of truth only as they satisfied your desires. So there was a neglect of the reality of truth, stressing rather the superficial approach. Here again was a lack of the development of sincere faith. Also, the intercepted Sagittarius in the eighth house shows the lack of appreciation for the higher values of truth, which could have been discovered through a sincere search in the field of metaphysics, philosophy, religion. This you neglected to do in the past. The rulership of Sagittarius by Jupiter implies the lack of development of wisdom in this respect.

Gemini intercepted in the third house, Sagittarius in the ninth.

There was a lack of follow-through when it came to acquiring knowledge. In the past, you did not find the proper means to communicate whatever you had to others. The sharing of knowledge — the cup running over — was lacking. There was mental aloofness rather than the sharing quality. Since this also deals with brothers and sisters, neighbors and relatives, the intercepted Gemini indicates that you did not develop mental communication in these relationships. There was no mental rapport established.

Sagittarius intercepted in the ninth house tells that in the past the lack of broad-mindedness was one of your characteristics. The Sagittarius intercepted shows you did not grant to others the freedom of expression, the right to opinion. The lack of the development of broad-mindedness showed itself in your dogmatic approach to religion, philosophy, psychology. Sagittarius intercepted in the ninth house stresses the need for tolerance and respect for the rights and opinions of others in this lifetime. It also stresses the fact that the higher mind was not utilized to its fullest in past lifetimes, nor did you incorporate the Christ principle. All knowledge, whether it was philosophy, religion, psychology, or any field of study, was self-centered. This again further emphasizes, as Gemini does in the third house, the need for sharing of knowledge. Knowledge was too often superficially acquired in the past and now there is need for sincerity.

Gemini intercepted in the fourth house, Sagittarius in the tenth.

These two intercepted should be very closely correlated. They are related as to how you influence and affect others in your immediate environment, whether it be home, neighborhood, job or wherever you might be. Gemini intercepted in the fourth house indicates that you did not influence other people in mental affairs. The responsibility of Gemini is to acquire knowledge, teach this knowledge to others, and demonstrate knowledge in a practical way. There was a lack of the ability to bring abstract thought down to the level of the understanding of the common man. You cannot influence others if they cannot understand what you are thinking or saying. Thought moves the world. This is the basic principle of creation, for all of creation is but the ideation of God. The world of ideas is involved with Gemini intercepted in the fourth house, as our ideas reflect what we are and how we guide and help others to find a meaning to life. Often this interception shows that, in the past, you lacked the patience to understand others on their level. There was a lack of the development of patience on your part.

The Sagittarius would represent the higher octave of Gemini, but here the influence was felt on a broader base, not just on your own personality or on the people with whom you came in contact on a daily basis. We are concerned here with public opinion, and advertising. The Sagittarius intercepted in the tenth house shows that your mind was not used to sway the minds of man. You neglected to develop a broad influence. Here again was the lack of a sense of responsibility to the world. It implies that you were more concerned with your own particular development and progress and less with the progress and development of others.

Gemini intercepted in the fifth house, Sagittarius in the eleventh.

Gemini intercepted in the fifth house, concerning your relationships with others, indicates that in the past you lacked a creative quality in relationships. All of life is a matter of relationships. Gemini intercepted shows that there was an aloofness in relationships. Were you concernned about other people? Did you have a mental awareness of others? In the past you could easily have dwelled in the ivory towers of activity and not enough in the mundane affairs of life. There was a paucity of feeling for the problems of other people.

Sagittarius intercepted in the eleventh house again indicates that in any relationship, whether with friends or social affairs, or in general relationships, you had to be the center of attention. Relationships were valued only insofar as they were an advantage for you. There was no selflessness in relationships. Any relationship was entered into purely from the viewpoint of personal gain, whether social, economic, or otherwise. The Sagittarius intercepted shows that you could not see the value of the proper development of relationships in your life. Friendships were superficial; therefore, there was no loyalty.

Gemini intercepted in the sixth house, Sagittarius in the twelfth.

This indicates that you did not employ patience in service to humanity. There was too much restlessness and impatience where people or the public were concerned. The Gemini quality would indicate that there was little sympathy or understanding given to the needs of the common man. You had little respect for social trends of the time. There could have been a tendency on your part to be coldly criticial of the masses. Here again is emphasized the lack of the development of feelings and emotions. Service was not rendered with feelings and understanding.

Sagittarius intercepted in the twelfth house directly relates to

the soul quality development and Karma. The self-centeredness of
the Sagittarius prevented you from becoming aware of your soul
qualities. You lacked the ability to relate to your fellow man and to
the cosmos. The "oneness" of universality was viewed through a
self-centeredness. You were your own universe, but the universe,
revolved around you and for your self. True spirituality was neglected. This also indicates that you lacked faith insofar as true
cosmic laws and principles were concerned.

Gemini intercepted in the seventh house, Sagittarius in the first.

This interception indicates a correlation between the proper
development of the "I" and the lack of proper development of the
"We". Gemini intercepted in the seventh house shows there was
not enough feeling and understanding in relationship to the "We"
concept. This lack would show itself in partnerships on all levels,
but most of all in partnership with life. You remained aloof from
life. Because it is in the third quartile, this interception implies that
you must project yourself into life itself. You did this in past lives
but it was done purely from a mental level rather than from one of
understanding. Again by reaction with Sagittarius in the first
house, this was done purely from the viewpoint of self-
centeredness rather than from the viewpoint of your relating to life.
In the past you did not develop the proper personality so that the
world would see you as you related to others. There was aloofness
on your part and you lacked warmth and sincerity. You may have
projected a dualistic type of personality. You presented yourself
one way but, actually, this was a false front or a facade for what
you were really like. It could imply, also, that you developed a sort
of mechanistic approach in presenting yourself to others. You were
accomodating. In other words, in a certain situation, you would
behave in one way, and in another situation, you would behave in
another way — whatever was expected of you. You had a mechan-
ical sort of approach, lacking sincerity. Underneath it all, you had
the reverse feelings. You could have had a cold personality, lend-
ing itself to snobbery, associating and presenting yourself to others
when it was to your advantage from a viewpoint of security or
material things.

Gemini intercepted in the eighth house, Sagittarius in the second.

The intercepted Gemini shows that your search for truth, your involvement in metaphysics, was purely intellectual. You had a cold, analytical approach. There was the lack of the development of compassion and understanding where truth was concerned. This is the house of higher values and you did not develop values on the highest possible level for truth per se. Also, since Gemini is ruled by Mercury, you did not develop the communication of knowledge where truth was concerned, here again indicating that you relegated it to the realm of the abstract rather than the concrete.

Sagittarius intercepted in the second house emphasizes values, but it is more concerned with the ego and the "I". You placed little value upon the proper development of self-awareness. There was little attention placed upon becoming aware of the value of self in relationship to life. Everything that you did in the past would have centered upon personal security, personal possessions. There was little acknowledgment of the fact that things are of value only as they are used in service to mankind. Here was the value of things for their own sake — not for the appreciation of how they could be used, or even from the viewpoint of appreciation of their beauty. Superficial values were the basis of the intercepted Sagittarius and it was a matter of "What's mine is mine" in the past. This location of the intercepted Sagittarius stresses the materialistic attitudes of the past at the neglect of the spiritual, whereas the Gemini intercepted stresses the abstract at the expense of the concrete.

Gemini intercepted in the ninth house, Sagittarius in the third.

Intercepted Gemini in the ninth house concerns the qualities of the higher mind and again stresses cold intellectual approaches when it came to higher learning and the higher mind. To you the Christ principle would have been a principle in theory only, not in application. There was little patience developed towards those who could not understand as clearly as you did. This interception indicates that you found it extremely difficult to communicate higher

knowledge or higher mind activities to others. You also lacked
tolerance for others who could not agree with your opinions.

Sagittarius intercepted in the third house shows that any educational endeavor was undertaken purely from the viewpoint of
your self-advancement. Relationships with neighbors, brothers and
sisters, existed only to serve your purpose. There was a false sense
of values where family connections were concerned. You only
communicated what was important to yourself in the past, not what
was important to others. Here again we stress the lack or neglect of
the sharing of knowledge in the past. One thing must be stressed
concerning sharing and that is this: the sharing of knowledge concerns not only bits of information or skills you develop, but also
the experiences in life which often teach more than academic
information.

Gemini intercepted in the tenth house, Sagittarius in the fourth.

An intercepted Gemini in the tenth house indicates that everything you did from the viewpoint of career did not incorporate the
feeling of contribution to the job. The job was only a means for
your personal achievement and security. Here is the Capricorn
influence as Capricorn rules the tenth house. It could imply that
your mental qualities were used only for whatever prestige you
could achieve, not for what you could contribute in new techniques
or new approaches. Often you only became involved out of necessity in positions of authority or careers. Perhaps you took the path
of least resistance.

Sagittarius intercepted in the fourth house implies that you did
not involve yourself with the affairs of mankind. Your philosophy
was "You made your bed, now lie in it." The intercepted Sagittarius shows your lack of developing the awareness of your responsibility to your fellowman — a refusal to accept the fact that
you *are* your brother's keeper, in that everything you do or say or
think influences every unit of manifested life in all kingdoms.

Gemini intercepted in the eleventh house, Sagittarius in the fifth.

Gemini intercepted in the eleventh house shows that relationships were based mainly on mental rapport. You were intolerant of those who might not have been as interesting or might not have known as much as you. You failed to see that you should have assumed the responsibility of mentally stimulating others and rasising the consciousness of others. You were the type of person who would ignore others less fortunate than you in mental agility and mental ability. Here was intellectual snobbery, and a failure on your part to communicate to others where levels of consciousness were involved. You failed to stimulate the imagination of others in the past and were too logical and unemotional in your relationships.

Sagittarius in the fifth house shows that you did not use mental creativity in developing relationships with others. Relationships were based upon what advantage they would be to you. It shows the superficiality of your friendships and loyalties. Wouldn't this also imply the lack of your development of the proper philosophy toward your relationship with others? Everything had to be the way *you* wanted. Relationships were a matter of taking rather than giving. This indicates your narrowness of self rather than an expansion of self.

Gemini intercepted in the twelfth house, Sagittarius in the sixth.

Gemini intercepted in the twelfth house shows that any attempt toward spirituality was made in a cold, intellectual, analytical way. True spirituality depends upon understanding and compassion — aligning yourself with higher forces. You failed to realize the value of soul qualities for these are not visible qualities. You were the type of person that would say "Show me." There was the lack of the development of your imagination to comprehend spiritual laws. The mental quality of Gemini interfered with your true attunement with humanity, creating a tendency to remain aloof from "the follies of the world." Gemini intercepted here shows that the mental level you possessed in the past could have mitigated some of that folly.

The Sagittarius intercepted in the sixth house shows that there was a lack of selfless service to the public. Here again any service that you would have rendered in the past would have been from the viewpoint of the advantages that you would receive. It was superficial service. It demonstrates that you did not relate to spirituality, universality, and brotherhood. Here discrimination entered into the picture. There was also a great deal of impatience with others. Sagittarius intercepted here shows that there was not the final completion or fulfillment of the "I Am" on your part, as the self related to the mundane affairs of life.

CANCER & CAPRICORN

Cancer intercepted in the first house, Capricorn in the seventh.

If you have Cancer intercepted in the first house, it indicates that in the past you neglected to develop the warm type of personality to which people could respond. There is a combination of the coldness of a Gemini and the domineering trait of a Leo which does not take into consideration other people. So Cancer seems to be sandwiched in between the qualities of these two signs. This is a result of neglecting to develop the feeling aspect in the past.

Capricorn in the seventh house also involves the conflict of identifying self with others, since the Capricorn tends to be conservative and prefers not to be too involved in the problems of other people. In both instances, you have the conflict between the development of the "I Am" and the "We" concepts.

Cancer intercepted in the second house, Capricorn in the eighth.

With this interception, the possessive quality of Cancer concerns the problem of materiality. Too much attention was placed upon materiality, indicating the neglect of the development of proper values where things were concerned. From a feeling viewpoint, a true Cancer would realize the value of things, money, possessions, as instruments through which they can help others in the trials and tribulations of everyday life. Here the Cancer contributes a selfishness and shows the neglect of the development of an unselfish nature.

Capricorn intercepted in the eighth house again demonstrates the conservative quality in that whatever the Capricorn did, his ultimate aim was for self-advancement. Here is the lack of the devlopment of a true perspective in life — an unawareness of the truths that underlie all manifested life. It indicates that the Capricorn in the past placed too much value upon materiality at the expense of spirituality.

Cancer intercepted in the third house, Capricorn in the ninth.

This interception indicates the neglect on the part of the Cancer in the past to incorporate true feelings when it came to communicating with others. In many ways this person had a cold approach which did not inspire others to feel at ease with him. Knowledge was gleaned for the sake of knowledge itself rather than for sharing it with others. Could this person have felt an identification of self with all of manifested life? It would hardly seem so.

Capricorn intercepted in the ninth house shows that knowledge was acquired merely from the viewpoint of how it would enhance his prestige. Knowledge itself represented a security to him, a means whereby he could establish himself in life economically, socially and spiritually. The Capricorn in the past neglected to utilize the higher mind concept, especially the Christ concept, in communicating ideas, philosophy, opinions. There was definitely a failure to communicate, and to develop a means of communicating on a higher level.

Cancer intercepted in the fourth house, Capricorn in the tenth.

Cancer in the fourth house emphasizes the Cancerean qualities of warmth, of relating to the public, since it is in its own house position. What it indicates from a reincarnation and Karma viewpoint is the neglect to assume the responsibility of having an affect upon others. We must never forget that Cancer is sandwiched in between Gemini and Leo and so this indicates the qualities of the person in this lifetime, having failed to develop the quality of inspiring confidence, inspiring the "father confessor" rapport with others.

The person in this lifetime would either be aloof from affecting other people constructively or would attempt to control other people who came into his environment.

The Capricorn intercepted in the tenth house would show the lack of awareness of the use of authority and position. Authority carries responsibilities. Leadership requires a strong sense of responsibilities. These were neglected in the past and the Sagittarius on the cusp of the tenth house indicates that the individual was concerned more with using authority to reflect himself and his position by always advancing himself even at the expense of others. The Aquarius on the other side of the Capricorn (since Capricorn is intercepted) would demonstrate that the humanitarian aspect was not incorporated in the Capricorn. We must always remember that a sign with its qualities is the result of the preceding sign's experiences and a forerunner of the succeeding sign. Each represents a preparation stage for the next and so this sandwiching-in tends to incorporate a little of the qualities of the signs that surround the intercepted sign. This can all be transmuted. It does not always have to be. When we become aware of our neglect in the past, by working harder at it in this lifetime, it can all be transmuted.

Cancer intercepted in the fifth house, Capricorn in the eleventh.

With Cancer intercepted, we are dealing with love affairs, children and creativity more than any other affair of the fifth house. In love affairs, for example, the intercepted Cancer demonstrates the lack of true affection, true caring. The tendency, perhaps, was to use the opposite sex for personal gratification. Would there have been a true relationship to children quality involved? I doubt it very much! There would not have been the inspirational type of creativity. Most creativity has to involve a feeling on the part of the artist for that which he creates. Something of himself must be projected into the ''child'' of his creative talents.

Capricorn intercepted in the eleventh house shows that the indivdual neglected to develop good relationships in the past. All of life is based on relationships. In fact, the entire zodiac represents our relationships to the planet Earth and on a greater zodiac level, the relationships of the planet Earth to the galaxy. With the intercepted Capricorn, there was a neglect in the past to develop an extroverted approach in relationships or contacts with people and with life. There was a lack of confidence in permitting the emotions to be involved in relationships. Involvement, per se, was lacking. The Capricorn failed to see that he could have been involved with life without being involved emotionally. There should have been a development of the quality of detachment which incorporates compassion and understanding, less the emotions.

Cancer intercepted in the sixth house, Capricorn in the twelfth.

Cancer in the sixth house shows that there was little attempt at giving service to others. There was an indrawn type of personality which did not incorporate soul qualities into the everyday affairs of life. The individual neglected to identify himself with social trends of the time and/or the needs of his fellow man. This location of Cancer represents the fulfillment of the "I", the harvest of all our experiences in the material world, but this person neglected to incorporate any feelings relating to his life experiences.

Now, Capricorn intercepted in the twelfth house shows the neglect of finalizing the concept of universality or at-one-ment with all levels of manifested life. Soul qualities were neglected in favor of the materialism involved with Capricorn. There should have been a rasising of the consciousness on the part of the Capricorn in the past from the level of materiality and security to that of spiritual reality.

Cancer intercepted in the seventh house, Capricorn in the first.

Cancer intercepted in the seventh house tells that there was a lack of development of consideration and concern for others. This would have demonstrated itself in any and all unions entered into by the native of the chart. Unions could easily have been entered into out of sheer necessity from the viewpoint of needing roots, a feeling of belonging, or of having to "run the show".

The Capricorn intercepted in the first house lends itself to the lack of an extroverted personality, a fear of allowing others to get close, to know the individual, of letting the world see you as you really were for fear of being taken advantage of. This would hardly be the person in the past who would have been the life of the party. Here is the observer of life instead of the participant in life.

Cancer intercepted in the eighth house, Capricorn in the second.

Cancer intercepted in the eighth house relates to the esoteric interpretation of the Moon, the natural ruler of Cancer. There was a failure or neglect on the part of the individual to integrate the outer and inner person through a search for Truth. The individual failed to regenerate the soul qualities for there was little value placed upon them. The Moon always indicates our purpose in life on an esoteric level, so the intercepted Cancer demonstrates that the individual neglected to fulfill his purpose in life insofar as cosmic law and cosmic principles were involved.

Capricorn intercepted in the second house implies the neglect of transmuting material values to spiritual values. The Capricorn neglected to use material possessions and finances in a proper way. They were secured more from the viewpoint of accumulation for self rather than for use. The accumulation of materiality was undoubtedly from the viewpoint of prestige and how others would look up to this person for his wealth and position.

Cancer intercepted in the ninth house, Capricorn in the third.

Here the intercepted Cancer shows that there was little development of knowledge on a broad basis. It shows that the individual did not have respect for other people's opinions and philosophies and could easily have been prejudiced in the past. Knowledge was for the sake of knowledge and lacked the feeling for sharing knowledge with others so that they could find their direction in life. The Cancer neglected to develop the concept of live and let live and the respect for other people's opinions.

With Capricorn intercepted in the third house, we are faced with the conservatism or reserve of the Capricorn. It could imply that the Capricorn neglected to develop the skills of higher knowledge by focusing instead upon skills which would grant security.

Since the third house is involved with communication, the intercepted Capricorn did not communicate whatever knowledge he
had or whatever skills he acquired. These were maintained purely
for self. He failed, also, to see that everyone in the world is his
brother and that we are all inter-related. Capricorn also failed to
develop patience and understanding where others were concerned.

Can   r intercepted in the tenth house, Capricorn in the fourth.

Cancer intercepted in the tenth house again shows that we are
dealing with authority and position, and by reaction to the fourth
house, how we influence and affect others. The Cancer here is in
the natural location or rulership of Capricorn so again we have the
lack of the development of an out-going type of personality. There
was an absence of charm in the personality, a lack of the warmth
that would attract others. There was little regard as to how the
person advanced himself. This advancement in the past could have
been done at the expense of others. Truly aware people do not like
to hurt others, but this quality was ignored in the past.

The Capricorn intercepted in the fourth house further implies
the lack of involvement in life insofar as how we influence and
affect those around us. The Capricorn was too involved with his
own immediate environment and his own self centeredness.

The Capricorn shows the lack of concern as to how others
regard him, and how he related to the problems of the world. His
world was confined to his immediate environment and there was
little projection of himself into the environment around him. Again
we must emphasize that life is a matter of relationships and in-
volvements.

Cancer intercepted in the eleventh house, Capricorn in the fifth.

The Cancer intercepted in the eleventh house shows the neglect of the feeling concept in relationships. Relationships would
resolve themselves as a matter of form. The normal Capricorn
embodies the world and encapsules many people and their problems. The intercepted Cancer in the eleventh house failed to to

this. Relationships were either selectively based or accompanied with little regard for the feelings of others, or they were undertaken for the opportunity to dominate others. The Capricorn in the fifth house shows the neglect of the development, or the value of, being a creative individual. It also shows that the individual pursued relationships and life from a materialistic, down-to-earth approach. He would have resisted change in his own life and would certainly not have taken a chance or embarked on a new course of activity that had any risk involved.

We must not only be creative in our relationships with others but in our approach to life. We can even relate this to the development of a skill or artistry, but a skill in some artistic pursuit which would encourage the creative talents to come forth. All this was neglected with Capricorn in the fifth house.

Cancer intercepted in the twelfth house, Capricorn in the sixth.

What we are dealing with here with Cancer intercepted in the twelfth house is the person's inability or lack of relating himself to the absolute or the infinite. True spirituality was neglected in the past. There was a failure to recognize the oneness that pervades the universe. There was the neglect of transmuting emotions to detachment which involves compassion and understanding, rather than relating emotionally to life. There was failure on the part of the Cancer to give selfless service or service for the sake of service, not just for the pat on the back or the approbation.

Capricorn intercepted in the sixth house emphasizes again neglect of involvement in service to the needs of the public. It shows the lack of the development of patience with those less fortunate than the Capricorn. There was also a lack of discretion. Discretion could very easily have been based upon false precepts. The opportunity for the finalization or the fulfillment of the "I" concept was either avoided or neglected since this fulfillment would have required participation in the lives of others. The Capricorn could easily have been instrumental in teaching others the meaning of life but neglected to do so.

LEO & AQUARIUS

Leo intercepted in the first house, Aquarius in the seventh.

If Leo is intercepted in your first house, one of the areas that you neglected in past lifetimes was that of leadership. You would have had the type of ego that was not used to its fullest so that you could assume the responsibility of leadership in a constructive manner. One of the areas in the spiritual development of mankind is involved with the use of authority, the use of leadership. There is pride and there is false pride, and this area, too, was neglected in the past. One of the qualities that you should have developed and incorporated in your personality was the quality of true humility. When we refer to humility, we do not mean humbleness, or a groveling type of individual. In the past, you should have developed a personality that would have made you a leader among men. You should have assumed a position of having influence upon others; you should have been the type of person who would seize the reins of organizations and direct activities in life. Leo is always involved with ego. By ego, we do not mean a conceited quality, but an awareness of self, because it is the ego that we function through in life, and the use of the ego in the experiences of life impresses the soul. This influences soul growth and soul development. All this was neglected in the past.

Leo intercepted also implies that no consideration was given to the feelings of others in the past. With an intercepted Leo, you must find the balance through Aquarius because the Aquarian quality of humanitarianism will offset the Leo quality of lack of consideration and concern for others.

With Aquarius intercepted in the seventh house, the "We" concept was limited, for you did not include the overall picture of all humanity and, in all probability, whatever development of the "We" concept was there, was there in a limited fashion — limited to those immediately connected to yourself. This also implies the lack of development of the Uranian principles of harmony/wisdom, the Christ principle. The intercepted Aquarius shows you neglected to devlop a broad perspective where life itself was concerned. Again, stress is placed upon the limiting of your concern for those in your immediate circle rather than extending your concern for life and partnership to all forms of existence.

Leo intercepted in the second house, Aquarius in the eighth.

Leo intercepted in the second house shows the lack of recognition or realization of the importance of the ego. You had very little value developed from a creative sense as well. You undoubtedly had many opportunities to be creative and placed little value upon it. Again, referring to the leadership quality of Leo, this intercepted condition indicates that you neglected to assume positions of leadership. A good example of this is that you could have been requested to be a chairman of a committee, of an activity, a drive, an organization, and you refused with "Let so-and-so do it." Incidently, Leo intercepted here also shows that you did not develop the proper techniques in establishing important and non-important values in life.

Aquarius intercepted in the eighth house would show that you placed little value upon the higher concepts. Since the beginning, the history of mankind is replete with examples of man's attempt to find Truth, and the intercepted Aquarius sign shows that because of poor values you did not search for Truth in the past. Man is always seeking to pierce the veil of the unknown. The intercepted condition here indicates non-curiosity rather than curiosity. There was lack of interest in higher truths and in the development of spirituality. The philosophical and intellectual aspects of life were sacrificed for material security.

Leo intercepted in the third house, Aquarius in the ninth.

Leo intercepted in the third house shows the lack of development of leadership in communication. You should have been the out-going individual who would share his knowledge and experiences with others. You could have had too much pride and introversion in the past. Since Leo is also connected with creativity, how creative were you in communicating yourself, your own awareness, your own self-identification with others? This location of the intercepted Leo implies that the completion of the "I" was not accomplished, nor did you show any self-identification in the past. The purpose of life experiences through the horoscope is to achieve the goal of each quartile and then balance each quartile with its opposite. Leo intercepted in the third house shows you failed in this balance and in the fulfillment of the goal of the first quartile.

Aquarius intercepted in the ninth house is of extreme importance since it is concerned with the higher self, the higher mind and the Christ principle. This emphasizes, very much, the neglect of mental qualities in the past. Your mind was dormant; it wasn't given the freedom of expression. Intellectual pursuits were neglected, and very possibly, philosophical and psychological approaches and interests were pushed aside by you for "practical" reasons — the spiritual sacrificed for the material. As the ninth house concludes the completion of the "We" concept, balance, here again, was not struck. The sign of Aquarius is the sign of humanitarianism and with an intercepted Aquarius in the ninth house, you neglected to relate to other units of life. You also neglected to identify the higher self and the higher mind as being channels for cosmic mind and cosmic influence.

Leo intercepted in the fourth house, Aquarius in the tenth.

With Leo in this location, it shows that you did not attempt to fulfill the "I" concept, insofar as the awareness of self was involved, in how you influenced or affected others. It was not your goal or ambition in past lifetimes to leave your "thumb print" in the annals of history. Everyone should leave his imprint on life. With Leo intercepted in the fourth house, you had little concern as to how you contributed to life and to the welfare of others. You remained ego-centered and did not extend your self out to others. There was a lack of feeling for the circumstances in which other people existed in life. If you rendered any service, it would have been from the viewpoint of how it would reflect back on you, whereas the service should have been "self-less", without hope of reward.

Aquarius intercepted in the tenth house, shows you could have been involved in great humanitarian movements but neglected to participate in such. On a broad perspective, Aquarius intercepted in the tenth house shows how little you influenced public opinion. This is the house of propaganda, the house of authority. It really was the neglect of the development of a technique whereby you could have influenced the thinking of people in the past, thereby having an affect upon social, political, economic, and religious trends.

Leo intercepted in the fifth house, Aquarius in the eleventh.

Leo intercepted in the fifth house is involved with creativity, children, love affairs. The Leo here shows you failed to develop creativity, artistically in relationships with others, or in thought. The Leo intercepted also shows you failed in your responsibilities where children were concerned. In love affairs, Leo intercepted here shows you did not take into consideration the feelings of others. You were the individual who had to have everything as he wanted it, when he wanted it, regardless of what activity was involved.

Aquarius intercepted in the eleventh house shows the neglect to develop the right relationships with others. These relationships should have been based on brotherhood and universality. Instead of your relating to all of mankind, the intercepted Aquarius shows a limited relationship which would be based purely upon selectivity, common interests, etc. This also shows your failure to prepare yourself for the ultimate fulfillment of the "We", as represented by the twelfth house.

Leo intercepted in the sixth house, Aquarius in the twelfth.

Leo intercepted in the sixth house tells that you neglected service to others. This service should have been given freely.

Anything you did was for approbation. In other words, there were strings attached to everything you ever did in the past. An intercepted Leo in the sixth house shows you had little affinity for, or identification with, the public. You even found it difficult to identify with your co-workers. This could result from the proud, domineering qualities of Leo which would affect those who worked with you or under you. This position of the intercepted Leo granted many opportunities in the past for leadership with the public or with your co-workers, but you evidenced too much self-concern, and too little concern for the welfare of others.

Aquarius intercepted in the twelfth house involves itself with the fulfillment of the "I". Here is the reaping of the harvest of your experiences in life. In the past you failed to fulfill the "I". The "I" remained as "I". You were ego-bound rather than being an individual who visualized himself or projected himself into the affairs of life and service to others. This is a very important location for Aquarius since we are concerned with the soul, Karma, the inner person, spirituality and spiritual initiations, and the fulfillment of the "We".

Leo intercepted in the seventh house, Aquarius in the first.

With Leo intercepted in the seventh house, we are involved with the lack of development of true spirituality and true brotherhood. You failed to see yourself as part of the ALL, thus neglecting to develop at-one-ment, which could have brought universality and oneness. Uranus rules Aquarius on an esoteric level and involves the higher self. This higher self is the essence of the soul, our SPIRIT. This is the Cosmic Root Substance and you failed to recognize this quality and its application to life. Here, too, is implied the failure to spiritualize your "Self", the failure of spiritual initiations. We are involved here with the neglect to develop the "We" concept at the expense of the "I". The old metaphysical concept, "in giving up all, one gains all", was not developed in the past. The intercepted Leo in the seventh house shows you did not relate to partnership in a positive manner, whether it was marriage, business or life itself. You did not develop the feeling concept where others were concerned. The authority and power of the Leo in the past came *out* of Leo rather than *through* Leo.

Intercepted Aquarius in the first house shows this lack of development since it implies that there was a great opportunity for you to develop a personality which would have incorporated a relationship to all of life. You could have been a great humanitarian but instead of giving of yourself, you took. You neglected to reflect the Aquarian concepts of the humanitarian harmony/wisdom. Aquarians should step forth in the world as personalities and reflect the future. There was too much tendency on your part to hold onto the past which is not the natural inclination for you. It also implies that there was a lack of self-discipline in life. You neglected to freely express the personality.

Leo intercepted in the eighth house, Aquarius in the second.

Here you neglected to assume leadership in the search for Truth, metaphysics, astrology. It could have been that your involvement was an ego-centered one; you took pride in being a knowledgeable person, in being an "authority". But you lacked the development of true values where Truth was concerned. You failed to reflect Truth.

The intercepted Aquarius in the second house emphasizes the neglect of values where mind was concerned. You placed little value upon brotherhood or spirituality and little value for the opinions of others. Values were more material than spiritual in the past so here again is the sacrifice of the spiritual for the matieral.

Leo intercepted in the ninth house, Aquarius in the third.

Leo intercepted in the ninth house again implies the acquisition of knowledge for the sake of knowledge or from intellectual curiosity. You neglected to communicate knowledge to others or to share experiences. The knowledge reflected only the Leo rather than the Leo reflecting the knowledge or wisdom. Wisdom was especially neglected, for wisdom implies application of knowledge to life. You did not develop respect or consideration for the opinions and thoughts of other people and so you lacked broadmindedness. This interception shows, also, that you failed to develop a suitable philosophy in the past.

Aquarius intercepted in the third house implies that you did not communicate the Aquarian principles of brotherhood, universality, spirituality. This shows, also, that you did not share any of this with others, if it existed at all. This interception indicates your neglect to develop any of these qualities or to identify self with these particular qualities or concepts.

Leo intercepted in the tenth house, Aquarius in the fourth.

Leo intercepted in the tenth house shows that you did not assume positions of authority and may even have accepted inferior positions rather than take on positions in which you would have to make decisions and deal with people.

You could have been the type of person who was afraid to use authority because you did not know *how* to use it. This could imply an inferiority complex in the past.

Aquarius intercepted in the fourth house shows your neglect to influence others constructively from the viewpoint of harmony/wisdom/love/humanitarianism. You could have been the withdrawn intellectual who failed to see that all knowledge carries an accompanying responsibility. Knowledge has to be applied to life, shared with others and used to help others find meaning to life. This interception shows that you neglected to do this.

Leo intercepted in the eleventh house, Aquarius in the fifth.

Leo intercepted in the eleventh house shows that, in your relationships with others, you failed to incorporate humility and a concern and consideration for others. You could have been a leader in social life and, by reaction to the fifth house, very creative in shaping and molding social activities, trends and thoughts. It could indicate that your relationships in life were geared to the presentation of self since all Leo's must be in the center of the stage. It shows that you failed to occasionally "take a back seat." The leadership involvement with others was neglected.

Aquarius in the fifth house shows that you could have been extremely creative from a humanitarian viewpoint. Intellectually, your mind could have known no limits and there would have been no boundaries to your mind's exploration. The world's progress has been marked by those who dared to think ahead, those who dared to be creative, and to visualize what *could* be. The intercepted Aquarius shows that these qualities were neglected. Your philosophy was "let things be as they are." In other words, too often you felt more secure with what you had and what *was*, rather than gamble on what could be.

Leo intercepted in the twelfth house, Aquarius in the sixth.

Since we are dealing with Karma and soul, the intercepted Leo shows that your ego failed to identify with Karma, failed to develop soul qualities as part of the Whole. Instead of seeing your self as just a grain of sand on the beach, you saw yourself as the beach. You failed to relate to universality, brotherhood, true spirituality, and you failed to fulfill the "We".

Aquarius intercepted in the sixth house shows that you failed to participate in life and in the affairs of mankind. You had little affinity for humanitarian movements or social trends, and you neglected the fulfillment of the "I" in service not only to the public but, by reaction to the twelfth house, to all humanity. There was the neglect of the development of harmony in life, the neglect of service to others, and above all, the neglect of the application of the Christ principle and the higher mind in service to others.

VIRGO & PISCES

Virgo intercepted in the first house, Pisces in the seventh.

Virgo intercepted in the first house shows your lack of a sincere type of personality in the past. You were superficial rather than sincere. You failed to develop discrimination insofar as your relationships to others were concerned. There was a lack of patience in the past and a failure to utilize your personality in service to others. Many times the Virgo quality of "teaching" can demonstrate itself through the personality. An interception of Virgo in the first house — the teaching element — shows it was lacking.

Pisces intercepted in the seventh house shows the lack of development of your responsibilties towards others and towards life. There was neglect in incorporating the elements of compassion and understanding. You demonstrated a lack of concern and consideration for others. Since Pisces is concerned with spirituality, the interception indicates that you did not attempt to become a spiritualized entity. There was little evidence in the past of any direction towards brotherhood and universality.

Virgo intercepted in the second house, Pisces in the eighth.

Virgo intercepted in the second house illustrates that you neglected to develop a sense of values in discriminating between what was important and what was not important in life. There could have been too much emphasis placed upon the everyday, picayune affairs of life and not enough attention upon the important aspects. There also could have been a superficiality in the type of values held by you in the past, with little or no attempt made to transmute these values into sincere or higher ones.

Intercepted Pisces in the eighth house shows the avoidance of the responsibility to search for the meaning to life, to find the Truth behind all of creation. The intercepted Pisces shows you had been exposed to metaphysical teachings or higher truth teachings but either ignored them or neglected to avail yourself of these teachings. Because of this, your life did not characterize the use of these principles. There could have been extreme understanding of the higher truth laws and principles, but the Piscean quality of laziness could have deterred you from involvement.

Virgo intercepted in the third house, Pisces in the ninth.

Virgo intercepted in the third house shows that you did not value education or that you did not attempt to acquire knowledge in the past. If you did acquire the knowledge, you failed to share it with others. You could also have spent a great deal of time in the pursuit of useless studies, or the frills of knowledge rather than the basics or definite skills. There was also a failure to communicate with others. Since this location of the intercepted Virgo represents the completion of the first quartile, it shows that there was a failure to become self-aware and the self-identification principle of the third house through Mercury also was neglected.

Pisces intercepted in the ninth house shows the neglect of the pursuit of higher education, the neglect of the use of the higher mind, the neglect of the development of a proper philosophy of life. The intercepted Pisces shows too passive an attitude where these qualities are concerned. There wasn't enough effort being exerted in the past to complete the third quartile concern with the ''We'' concept. This prevented you from identifying with all of manifested life. If, in the past, you involved yourself with the higher mind, higher education, or the Christ principle, you certainly did not apply it to life and did not communicate it in any fashion.

Virgo intercepted in the fourth house, Pisces in the tenth.

The service aspect of Virgo was neglected here, for the fourth house tells you where you can be of service to others and how you can, through this service, influence others. You failed to develop the proper auric field so that you might have created a force field which would benefit anyone with whom you came in contact. The fourth house always requires a great deal of understanding and patience in your contacts with others and this, too, was not a pronounced quality in the past. A question might arise here as to whether or not the intercepted Virgo might indicate a lack of success in properly counselling others who might have sought your advice.

The intercepted Pisces in the tenth house indicates the failure to assume the responsibility of the proper use of authority in the past. You could easily have been a politician, a priest, or a person in high position in a career or profession. There is an accompanying responsiblity to position and the intercepted Pisces indicates that you could have accepted position but did not discharge the duties of the position efficiently. It could also imply that there was very little personal ambition in the past. It is extremely important, with the intercepted Pisces here, to also include the fact that the mid-heaven is the area through which cosmic sustainment comes to humanity. Pisces as the indicator of high spirituality would show by its intercepted situation that you failed to be a channel through which cosmic energy could be used for mankind. This is also involved with the cosmic pattern of the evolution of the planet Earth.

Virgo intercepted in the fifth house, Pisces in the eleventh.

We are involved here with the lack of the development of the creative talents. Creativity can be artistic or it can be in the manner in which we relate to others. The intercepted Virgo indicates that you may have used very superficial tactics in developing relationships and could have been a pseudo-intellectual in artistic pursuits. The artistic pursuits of the Virgo would tend more toward writing rather than an art such as painting or sculputure. Since this is the natural home of Leo, you may have been involved, in the past, in drama or theatrical pursuits, but it was the glamor aspects more than anything else that served as your incentive. You may have have had a lack of patience in dealing with children or a lack of discrimination in love affairs. The critical aspect of Virgo would be much involved in all of the affairs of the fifth house.

Pisces intercepted in the eleventh house shows that you did not develop the proper relationships with people. It indicates that your social life was a surface type of social life. Little value was placed upon friendship itself. You may have been the "fair-weather" type of friend in the past. By reaction to the Virgo, the Pisces intercepted here tells that there was a lack of discrimination in the choice of friends.

Virgo intercepted in the sixth house, Pisces in the twelfth.

Virgo intercepted in the sixth house shows you did not develop the quality of service. Virgos tend to be rather health-conscious and the intercepted Virgo could indicate that there was a lack of concern for health, bringing in the opposite extreme of the normal quality of Virgo. This location of Virgo relates to the end of the second quartile which concerns itself with the fulfillment of the "I". The "I" can only be fulfilled as it is applied to the experiences of life and in this the Virgo failed. There was not that application and so you will reap a poor harvest in this lifetime because of this failure. This location of the intercepted Virgo doubly emphasizes the necessity of the "teacher" and shows you could have had many opportunities to teach but failed to accept the responsibilities.

The intercepted Pisces in the twelfth house is the one location which indicates that a major spiritual initiation was "flubbed". This was mainly due to the fact that the Pisces failed to accept the responsibility of the awareness of true spirituality, failed to understand universality and brotherhood. There was also, by reaction to the sixth house, the failure of unselfish service to mankind.

Virgo intercepted in the seventh house, Pisces in the first.

Intercepted Virgo in the seventh house shows that the poor judgment and critical attitude of the Virgo were deterrents to a full realization of the third quartile concept of "We". It indicates that there was a great deal of superficiality, a lack of sincerity and purpose. The intercepted Pisces in the first house shows the lack of development of a positive, strong personality. You could have

been a passive person — a Mr. Milquetoast — in a past lifetime.
Here again we are concerned with the development of the "I"
concept and an intercepted Pisces in the first house shows the
failure to identify self and self-awareness. You could have been the
floundering person in the past, the fluttering, weak individual.

Virgo intercepted in the eighth house, Pisces in the second.

We are concerned here with the lack of development of the
practical mind where higher truth or the search for truth was
involved. Mercury rules Virgo and is the planet of the practical
mind, so the intercepted Virgo indicates the failure to bring
abstractions, truth, down to practical levels. You also failed to
teach these truths to others. The superficiality of Virgo is always
present and the intercepted condition could indicate a superficial
approach to finding truth. There could have been a lack of dis-
cernment on your part to distinguish between truth and untruth.
Also there would have been a lack in the development of higher
values concerning spirituality and intellectual activities.

Pisces intercepted in the second house shows the avoidance of
establishing values on a mundane level. This would be especially
true concerning material things. Here the intercepted Pisces could
imply that you were the type of person who did not know how to
handle money, who lacked respect for it, and did not learn the
proper use of material possessions.

Virgo intercepted in the ninth house, Pisces in the third.

The intercepted Virgo again emphasizes the lack of development of a practical application of skills, higher knowledge,
the Christ Consciousness in the daily experiences of life. Here
again poor judgment, poor discrimination, could have caused you
to pursue frilly-type educational courses, not realizing the values
involved in a more serious pursuit of knowledge. Your philosophy
of life would have been a superficial one. You could have been the
religious person who was religious "only from the teeth out," who

would give lip service to religious beliefs rather than actually exemplifying them. You failed to allow the mind to freely express itself and to allow others the same liberty.

The intercepted Pisces in the third house shows the lack of development of a body of knowledge which could be shared with others and the failure to communicate knowledge to others.

You lacked the understanding of the value of educational activities. You were the type of student whose involvement in school centered around the social life rather than the acquisition of skills or knowledge.

Virgo intercepted in the tenth house, Pisces in the fourth.

This interception could indicate that you were the type of person who did not develop tact and diplomacy in the use of authority in the past. Could you also have been the type of person who, in attempting to establish a career for himself, lacked the proper discrimination as to what career would offer him the best channel through which he could make the greatest contributions? Perhaps you selected your profession from the viewpoint of self-advancement rather than for what you could contribute. The improper use of authority is also indicated with this interception.

Intercepted Pisces in the fourth house shows that you did not assume your responsibilities in terms of how you influenced and affected others. On a purely mundane level, the interception shows indifference on your part to establish good home conditions. Would you not have been the type of person whose personality, habits and personal appearance, would create lack of trust on the part of others relying on you for help? Would you have assumed responsibilities in your own life? You failed to develop spirituality in yourself which would encourage others to seek you out for counsel, guidance or advice. You were the type of person who would not want to be bothered with other people's problems, would not like to listen to their troubles, would not lend a willing shoulder upon which others could pour their problems and troubles.

Virgo intercepted in the eleventh house, Pisces in the fifth.

The intercepted Virgo shows the lack of discrimination on your part in choosing the right type of social life and the correct associations. Discrimination can be very constructive when used properly. The lack of discrimination can often result in disaster. The intercepted Virgo shows you did not develop patience or understanding in your relationships with others. Most charts with Virgo on the cusp of the eleventh house indicate a type of person whose home is a social center. But the intercepted Virgo would indicate that you did not establish the type of environment which would encourage others to come to your home. It also shows that instead of being of service to others, you were the type of person who used others, and friendship was based on benefits to self. The intercepted Pisces in the fifth house shows the avoidance or lack of development of creativity, creative talents, creative skills, creative approaches to life itself. On a mundane level, the intercepted Pisces shows you may have been the type of parent who nagged children rather than assuming the responsibilities of rearing them properly. With an intercepted Pisces in the fifth house, you may also have been the type of person who tended to get involved in love affairs which ended disastrously. This could show deceit on your part, or being subject to deceit. Being subject to deceit would be a reaction to the intercepted Virgo in the eleventh — a result of poor discrimination.

Virgo intercepted in the twelfth house, Pisces in the sixth.

An intercepted Virgo here indicates a lack of a true sense of service in the past. Service would have been given from the viewpoint of rewards, gratuities — you would have been the type of person who gave but always with strings attached. There was a superficial attitude in your relationships. You would have been a surface humanitarian who, deep down, entertained much prejudice or was very criticial of others. There was a tendency to be too quick to judge others and a failure to relate the soul relationship of self to cosmic soul and to the soul of your fellow man.

Intercepted Pisces in the sixth house shows the lack of development of assuming the responsibility of service. There was not enough sympathy developed in the awareness of the needs of others. Here again we are involved with lack of spirituality, lack of the development of the sense of universality and one-ness. Sympathy in the past could have been sentimentality, which is the lowest rung on the ladder of sympathy and is usually based on emotions. In terms of health, the intercepted Pisces shows you had a lack of regard for physical well-being. You could have demonstrated this in the lack of personal hygiene, the lack of proper eating habits, of regulating work, rest and sleep. There could have been a tendency to over-indulge in alcohol and a tendency toward being an escapist when it came to facing the realities of life.

Loretta

♓ in 4th / ♍ in 10th page 53.

Brian

♎ in 3rd / ♈ in 9th page 12